CHANGING THE GAME

Asian Pacific American Female Athletes

MIA WENJEN

Asian American Female Athletes Who Have Changed the Game

When you think of Asian American female athletes, does anyone come to mind? Perhaps recent Olympians such as gold medalist Chloe Kim for snowboarding, four-time Olympian Julie Chu for ice hockey, or Natasha Kai-Marks for soccer. But there are many Asian American female athletes who, despite reaching a high level of success, are not well known. Many have also overcome racism and poverty to excel in their sport. Let's take a look at some of the trailblazers who have paved the way.

Image credits: © Alamy, Associated Press, Dreamstime, iStock, Shutterstock, and courtesy of EJL Smith

To order more copies of *Changing the Game*, please visit MiaWenjen.com.

Book produced by 22MEDIAWORKS, INC.
www.22MediaWorks.com
lary@22MediaWorks.com

President LARY ROSENBLATT
Design and Production FABIA WARGIN DESIGN
Writer MIA WENJEN
Editor SUSAN ELKIN
Copy Editor LAURIE LIEB
Photo Research DAVID PAUL PRODUCTIONS

Julie Chu

(Eun Jung)
EJ Lee Smith

She is a basketball superstar that few know about.

"The best female point guard I've ever seen."

—Dale Brown,
Louisiana State University Men's Head Coach

Have you had to hide your sport from a parent?

EJ's father did not know that she played basketball until she was on national TV! EJ Lee Smith was one of the best college basketball players to ever play the sport!

Standing at just five feet, six inches, EJ Lee Smith did not look like a basketball star. But on the court, she seemed to have eyes in the back of her head. As a point guard for Northeast Louisiana University (now the University of Louisiana at Monroe), EJ found a way to reach her forwards with no-look lob and behind-the-back passes. She would rack up points as well, averaging 18.8 points per game during her four years in college. EJ was named the No. 1 point guard in the nation in **1986**, and she held records at the university for the most free throws made, most assists, most steals, most games played, and highest assist average.

Born in Gimje, South Korea, EJ was the youngest of five children. When her school decided to start a basketball team, EJ's mother, a short-distance runner, decided to let her play but kept it from her husband, who didn't think girls should participate in sports.

After graduating from Soongeui High School, EJ played for Korea's semiprofessional league before accepting a scholarship at Louisiana. She arrived on campus not speaking a word of English. She became one of the most popular students on campus, known for her warm personality as well as her basketball skills.

After graduating from college in 1986, EJ played basketball professionally in Sweden and Italy. She was named Most Valuable Player for both seasons in Europe.

Teresa Weatherspoon, four-time WNBA All-Star and Olympic gold medalist, described EJ as "one of the greatest [point guards] that I've played against."

After coaching for her alma mater, EJ became the head girls' coach at River Oaks High School in Monroe, Louisiana. One of the greatest point guards ever to play college basketball, she is also, equally, a hidden figure ahead of her time.

Chloe
Kim

PyeongChang 2018™

1

Do you speak one language?

Korean American athlete Chloe Kim was born in California and spoke both Korean and English fluently. When she was eight, she moved to Geneva to learn French, her third language. Even though she was very young, her parents did not go with her. She lived with her aunt and trained with the Swiss national snowboarding team. When she won gold at the South Korea Winter Olympics, she was able to give interviews in Korean.

Chloe Kim is the youngest snowboarder to win an Olympic gold medal. She was just 17 years old when she landed back-to-back 1080-degree spins in the women's snowboard halfpipe event at the 2016 Winter Olympics in PyeongChang, South Korea.

Chloe's parents, Jong Jin Kim and Boran Yun Kim, immigrated from South Korea to the United States in 1982. Chloe was born and raised in California. Her father introduced her to snowboarding when she was four years old and put her on the snowboarding team at Mountain High Resort when she was six because it was less expensive than lessons.

> "Just because I'm young doesn't mean I didn't work hard to get where I am."
>
> —Chloe Kim

After training two years in Switzerland, Chloe returned to the United States and continued her training at Mammoth Mountain. She began competing at a professional level when she was 12.

Chloe earned a place on the U.S. Olympic team in 2014, at age 13, but the minimum age to compete was 15. At the X games in 2015, she became the youngest snowboarder, male or female, to win gold.

Competing in the 2016 Olympics was a homecoming of sorts. Chloe's relatives in South Korea were able to watch her compete for the first time. Able to bridge both cultures, Chloe gave interviews in fluent Korean.

After the Olympics, Chloe chose to focus on academics at Princeton University. But snowboarding fans needn't fear. She still plans to perfect her double cork front-side 1080!

Miki Gorman

Do you like to run? Michiko "Miki" Suwa Gorman started
distance running as an adult and became the best in the world. She
is the only female runner to have won both the Boston Marathon and
the New York City Marathon two times each.

She was born in Qingdao, China, on August 9, 1935. She attended
an elite school for the Japanese living there. Miki was one of the top
runners on the school track team. When she was ten years old, her
family returned to Japan. Her family evacuated to the countryside
to escape the bombing of Tokyo during World War II. Life was hard
then. There wasn't enough food to eat, and Miki was hungry every day.

At age 28, Miki moved to the United States with
just $10 in her pocket to work as a nanny for the
family of a U.S. military officer. She also took secre-
tarial classes at Carlisle Commercial College in
Pennsylvania. After completing her degree, she
relocated to Los Angeles for a job. It was there
that she met and married Michael Gorman, a
businessman.

To expand her social circle, she joined the
Los Angeles Athletic Club (LAAC). For the first
time since living in China, Miki started running
again. Fiercely competitive, she quickly improved
through intense training.

It wasn't until 1972 that women were allowed
to compete in races that were more than one and a half
miles. In 1973, Miki decided to run in the Culver City Marathon.
She won with a time of 2:46:32, six seconds shy of the world record.

Miki Gorman would make history in 1974, winning the Boston
Marathon with a time of 2:47:11. In 1977, she won both the Boston
Marathon and the New York City Marathon, becoming the first
runner, male or female, to win both events in the same year.

"All I want to do is speed, speed."
—*Miki Gorman*

Victoria Manalo Draves

Would you change your name for your sport?

Vicki Draves wasn't allowed to train at the Fairmont Hotel Swimming and Diving Club in San Francisco because of her ethnic last name. She had to change her name to her mother's maiden name to get access to a swimming pool.

Victoria "Vicki" Draves was born to be a winner. Her maiden name, Manalo, means "to win" in Tagalog, a language widely spoken in her father's native Philippines. She lived up to her name, garnering many firsts. She was the first woman to win two gold medals at a single Olympics, the first Asian American to medal at the Olympics, and the first Filipino to win a gold medal.

Born in 1924, Vicki grew up in San Francisco as part of an interracial family. Her Filipino father, Teofilo Manalo, was a chef, houseboy, and musician. Her English mother, Gertrude Taylor, worked as a maid.

Vicki wanted to be a ballerina but her family didn't have money for lessons. Instead, she channeled her grace into diving, which she discovered at 16 years old. At that time, most swimming pools in America were designated as "whites only."

She was the first woman to win Olympic gold in both the 10-meter platform and the 3-meter springboard events.

"**I was so nervous that I would shake before each dive.**"

—*Vicki Draves*

For one day a month, the day before the pool was drained and cleaned, the pool would be opened to non-whites. To allow her to train, her coach had to form a club just for her, the Patterson School of Swimming and Diving. Her father wasn't able to watch her dive in her early years because he was barred from the pools for being Filipino.

Vicki competed in her first national championship after just three years of training. At the age of 19, Vicki met Lyle Draves, a diving coach who taught her platform diving in addition to springboard. She married him in 1946. Vicki was ready for international competition, but the 1944 Olympic Games were canceled due to World War II. She had to wait until the 1948 London Olympics.

On August 3, 1948, Vicki, at age 23, became the first Filipino to represent the United States. She won her first gold medal in the women's three-meter springboard event. She would add another gold in the ten-meter platform event. Her achievement was noted in *Life* magazine, which named her one of the top two American athletes of the London Olympic games.

Evelyn Tokue Kawamoto

Would you swim in a ditch because you didn't have access to a swimming pool? Evelyn Kawamoto was part of the Three-Year Swim Club created by coach Soichi Sakamoto. The name reflected his goal to get his swimmers on the Olympic team in just three years. They trained in an irrigation ditch using new techniques such as interval training and pacing using a metronome. Evelyn was one of 14 champions to come out of his program.

At just 18 years old, Evelyn Kawamoto was the first Japanese American to win an Olympic medal. She won two bronze medals at the 1952 Olympic Games in Helsinki for the 400-meter freestyle and the 100-meter freestyle relay.

Evelyn was born in Honolulu, Hawaii. Her single mother, Sadako Kawamoto, earned a meager living by taking in laundry. Evelyn started swimming when she was nine years old. Under Sakamoto's tutelage, she began breaking American swimming records. At age 14, she broke two records on the same day, for the women's 300-meter individual medley and the 200-meter breaststroke.

Evelyn was part of a controversial decision about judging and timing in swimming history. At the Women's Nationals in 1950, she tied with Marge Hulton in the 200-meter breaststroke. The three timers who judged their event thought that both swimmers had the exact same time. It was the first dead heat in the history of Amateur Athletic Union swimming. Unable to declare a winner, the judges awarded both Evelyn and Marge a hybrid gold and silver medal. This controversy prompted the introduction of a new electronic judging system for swimming that eventually evolved into the modern touch pad.

Evelyn married her childhood sweetheart, Ford Konno. He also trained under Soichi Sakamoto and won two gold and two silver Olympic medals himself. Extremely modest, Evelyn rarely spoke about her swimming career. In 2000, she was inducted into the Hawaii Sports Hall of Fame.

The Pacific Citizen viewed Kawamoto as "probably the greatest Nisei girl athlete in history."

Julie Chu

Would you join a boys' team as the only girl?

When Julie Chu started playing hockey in 1990, she was one of only 5,000 or so girls in the United States to take up the sport. She had to join a boys' team because there weren't any leagues for girls. In fact, as a youth player, the only other girl that she would see in an entire season was her sister! In 1992, women's hockey became an Olympic sport and now there are more than 60,000 girls playing hockey in the United States. Julie is a pioneer in the sport, both as an athlete and as someone who helped to grow the sport.

Julie Chu is the first Asian American female to compete for the United States in the Winter Olympics in a sport other than figure

"People used to say girls shouldn't play hockey. Well, that's starting to disappear. It's the same thing with cultures or ethnicities and who should be doing what sport. Well, let people pursue what they're passionate about—that's how it should be."

—*Julie Chu*

skating. She was selected as the best female collegiate hockey player in the United States in 2007, winning the Patty Kazmaier Award. Julie competed in four Olympics, earning three silver medals and one bronze, and won five world championships.

Ice hockey wasn't the first sport that Julie played. Julie grew up playing soccer. When her brother started playing hockey, Julie and her sisters were enrolled in figure skating classes.

Julie found the graceful moves of figure skating frustrating and preferred watching the boys on the rink playing hockey. It looked fast-paced and fun. After two months, she switched. She was just 8 years old.

She went on to dominate in ice hockey, making the national team for the first time at age 18 while a senior in high school. After graduating from high school, Julie played for Harvard and became the all-time leading scorer in National Collegiate Athletic Association (NCAA) history with 284 points.

During her time in college, she also competed in her first Olympics. She went on to compete in four Olympics—2002, 2006, 2010, and 2014—becoming the second-most decorated U.S. female athlete in Olympic Winter Games history.

Julie continues to give back to her sport as a coach. She helped guide the University of Minnesota Duluth to an NCAA victory in 2008 as an assistant coach and went on to coach at Union College and Concordia University.

Natasha Kai-Marks

Have you ever returned to something that you quit? Natasha Kai-Marks reached the ultimate goal for most athletes, winning an Olympic gold medal for soccer. After competing as a professional soccer player for three years, she quit. But something drew her back to the game.

Natasha Kai-Marks is one of only 15 women of color to make the full U.S. women's national soccer team during its first three decades of existence. Between 2006 and 2011, she scored 24 goals in 63 appearances for the U.S. national team. Tasha was also a member of the USA Women's Rugby 7s team.

Born in Kahuku, Oahu's north shore known for its big waves, Natasha grew up surfing but also played soccer, volleyball, basketball, and ran track and field. Natasha grew up in a close-knit family with five younger siblings. Her father, "Uncle Benny" Kai, played the guitar and ukulele as a host of the lūʻau at the Polynesian Cultural Center in Oahu. Tasha learned ukulele as well.

She won an Olympic gold medal for women's soccer but only played community-based soccer as a child.

After competing for a World Cup in 2007 and winning an Olympic gold medal in 2008, Natasha played soccer professionally for Sky Blue FC and then for Philadelphia Independence of Women's Professional Soccer. Injuries and burnout sidelined her. When the American Professional Soccer League folded in 2011, she decided that she was done with soccer.

When her father was diagnosed with cancer, his dying wish was for her to return to soccer. It took Natasha three years, training seven days a week, to return to full strength. She returned to her old team, Sky Blue FC, in 2016. She also played for the Los Angeles Galaxy.

The first player from Hawaii to make the full U.S. national women's soccer team, Natasha continues to play professionally, coaches, and advocates for mental health support of elite athletes.

"The highlight of my career was going to the Olympics. That will always be a highlight."

—*Natasha Kai*

She was the youngest player to qualify for a USGA amateur championship and the first female to qualify for an adult men's USGA championship.

Michelle Wie

Would you compete against adults? Michelle Wie was used to playing golf against adults. When she was 10, she was the youngest player to qualify for a U.S. Women's Amateur Public Links championship. Because she hit the ball really far, she knew that she could compete against men too.

When Michelle won the U.S. Women's Amateur Public Links at age 13, she became the youngest player—male or female—to win a United States Golf Association (USGA) adult event. She turned professional two years later. With five victories on the Ladies Professional Golf Association (LPGA) tour, including the **2014** U.S. Women's Open, her story as a golf prodigy is still being written.

Michelle was introduced to golf at the age of four. Her mother, Bo, played golf competitively in South Korea, winning the women's amateur golf championship in 1985. Her father, Byung-wook Wie, also an immigrant from South Korea, taught travel industry management at the University of Hawaii.

Michelle dominated the junior amateur tours. Because she could drive the ball nearly 300 yards, she could successfully compete against boys and adults. At age 14, Michelle became the first female to qualify for an adult men's USGA championship, the U.S. Amateur Public Links. When she competed in the Sony Open, she became the youngest female to compete on the men's PGA Tour. Though she missed the second-round cut by one stroke, she still beat 46 men!

Still, her golf career was plagued by medical problems. She battled joint inflammation in her hands, arthritis in both wrists, and bursitis in her left hip. She also broke her right wrist and hand in a car accident. These problems all affected her golf swing.

In June 2020, Michelle and her husband, Jonnie West, welcomed a baby girl. Since then, she has returned to competitive golf.

"It's a very hard game, a brutal game. But I still love the challenge."

—*Michelle Wie*

19

Kristi Yamaguchi

Did you know that ice skating can correct clubfoot?

Clubfoot is a condition causing a newborn baby's foot or feet to be twisted out of position, making it hard to walk normally. Kristi Yamaguchi started ice skating at the age of six as a form of physical therapy. Not only did ice skating correct her condition, but she fell in love with the sport.

She was born with two club feet.

Ice skating is a form of therapy.

Kristi Yamaguchi was the first Asian American to win Olympic gold in figure skating, winning the figure skating singles in **1992**. She is also a two-time singles world champion (1991 and 1992) and a pairs skater two-time national champion with Rudy Galindo (1989 and 1990).

Kristi was born in Hayward, California, in 1971 to Jim and Carole Yamaguchi. Both her parents had been interned during World War II because they were Japanese American. Kristi's maternal grandfather, George Doi, was an infantry lieutenant in the U.S. Army who served in Europe even as his wife and children were incarcerated.

Kristi started competing in junior high school in singles as well as in pairs with partner Rudy Galindo. They won the U.S. pairs championship in **1986** and again in 1990. Kristi also placed second in singles.

For two years, Kristi was the first U.S. female figure skater to medal in both singles and pairs, but in 1990, at age 18, she decided to focus on singles. It was the right choice. Kristi won her first world championship title in 1991 in singles figure skating. At the 1992 Olympic Winter games in Albertville, France, Kristi won a gold medal in women's singles.

After bringing home her gold medal, Kristi founded the Always Dream Foundation. Her charity provides free e-readers and tablets to help underserved children learn to read. Kristi was inducted into the U.S. Olympic Hall of Fame in **2005**.

"My grandfather didn't talk much about World War II, but he let me know how proud he was to see me make it as an Asian-American representing the United States."

—*Kristi Yamaguchi*

Amy Chow

"I hope that with the success of Asian Americans in athletics more and more Asian parents put their kids into sport or encourage the sporting side of their life as well as the academic side."

—*Amy Chow*

Sydney 2000

Have you tried to keep your balance while walking on the edge of a curb? It's easy to pretend that you are on the balance beam! Now, imagine that you are starting your routine on the balance beam, but you fall and hit your head. This happened to Amy Chow during the Olympic trials. Even though she was in pain, she got back on the balance beam and completed her routine. Falling didn't rattle her and she ended up making the team!

Amy Chow is best known as a member of the "Magnificent Seven," along with Amanda Borden, Dominique Dawes, Shannon Miller, Dominique Moceanu, Jaycie Phelps, and Kerri Strug. In **1996**, they brought home the first U.S. team gold medal in gymnastics. She also won a silver medal for her performance on the uneven bars. In **2000**, Amy returned to the Olympics where the U.S. gymnastics team was ultimately awarded the bronze medal.

Born to Nelson and Susan Chow, immigrants from Guangzhou, China, and Hong Kong respectively, Amy began taking gymnastic classes at the age of three. At 11 years old, she started to compete nationally. Gymnastics wasn't Amy's only sport. She competed as a pole vaulter and a diver in high school, and continued diving at Stanford University.

Amy contributed a nearly flawless performance on the uneven bars at the 1996 Summer Olympics in Atlanta, Georgia, scoring a 9.837. She earned a silver medal for her individual performance. Nicknamed "The Trickster" for her ability to pull off extremely difficult moves with ease, she has two gymnastic skills named after her, the Chow/Khorkina and the Chow II, both on the uneven bars.

After a visit to her pediatrician when she was a young child, Amy told her mom that she wanted to be a doctor. Amy now practices as a pediatrician in Northern California after graduating from Stanford Medical School.

She is the first Asian American to win gold in Olympic gymnastics.

Anona Napoleon

Have you ever tried to ride a wave? You can do that with your body, a boogie board, or a surfboard. Anona Napoleon loved riding the waves. She surfed and kayaked with her brothers. When she as 19 years old, a diving accident left her paralyzed. Doctors did not think she would recover. One year later, however, she made a full recovery. She competed in the 1961 International Mākaha Surfing Competition and was crowned the winner!

A champion surfer and kayaker, Anona Napoleon was born in 1941 into a celebrated Hawaiian surfing family and grew up tagging along after her older brothers and their friends. As a teenager, she was one of the few girls who would surf the big waves. In 1964, Anona married Nappy Napoleon, who was also a champion outrigger canoe paddler and steersman.

After a diving accident, she was told that she would never walk again. One year later, she became a surfing champion.

Anona was also a champion paddler. She narrowly missed making the 1960 and 1964 Olympic two-person kayaking team. In 1975, her team was one of two all-female teams to successfully cross the Ka'iwi Channel—41 miles of dangerous open ocean—in the Molokai Hoe outrigger canoe competition. Her team also won the women's world championship of paddling, Nā Wāhine o Ke Kai, in 1979, 1987, 1988, and 1989. In 1988, she came in first at the International Polynesian Canoe World Sprint Championships.

Not only a gifted athlete, Anona also excelled in the classroom. She earned a PhD in education at the University of Hawaii, where her work focused on Hawaiian culture. She brought Ho'oponopono, the art of peacemaking, into the classroom and adapted this concept to learning and mentoring methods.

A trailblazer in both the classroom and the ocean, Anona Napoleon was inducted into the Hawaiian Waterman Hall of Fame in 2014.

"It's about aloha. Be humble, show your aloha freely to everyone, and above all, have fun."

—*Anona Napoleon*

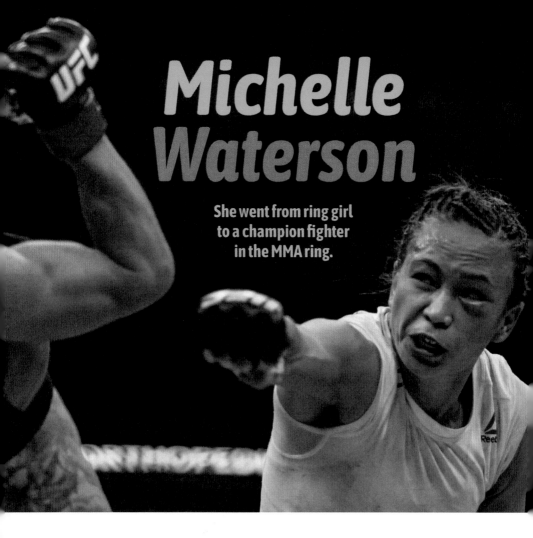

Michelle Waterson

She went from ring girl to a champion fighter in the MMA ring.

Have you ever watched a sport and wished you could try it? When Michelle Waterson graduated from high school in 2004, there were no women fighting professionally in Mixed Martial Arts (MMA). Her only opportunity was as ring girl, the woman who holds up a sign between rounds to show the number of the upcoming round. But she was more interested in being inside the octagon than outside it. Michelle trained in a variety of martial arts and sought out amateur fights. When the Ultimate Fighting Championship (UFC) opened up competitions to women in 2007, Michelle was ready and turned professional.

Michelle was an Invicta Fighting Championships Atomweight champion from 2013 to 2014. She currently fights in the UFC strawweight division at 115 pounds.

She was born in Colorado Springs to Robert and Metta Waterson. Her father is of European descent, and her mother is from Thailand. Michelle was introduced to martial arts through her older brother, who took karate classes. Following in his footsteps, Michelle earned a black belt in American freestyle karate. She went on to study wushu, Brazilian jiu-jitsu, boxing, and wrestling.

A strong student in high school ranking 10th in her class, Michelle nonetheless felt lost in college as a freshman at the University of Denver. When her mother took her to Thailand to visit family, Michelle studied Muay Thai kickboxing at Sityodtong camp in Pattaya. After her Muay Thai training, Michelle decided to pursue a career as a mixed martial arts fighter.

After more than 24 fights, including 17 wins with three by knockout, Michelle's career took another turn when she gave birth to a daughter, Araya, on March 18, 2011.

Nine months later, Michelle returned to the octagon, defeating Diana Rael in the first round. In **2016**, Michelle's balancing act as a mother and MMA fighter was chronicled in the documentary *Fight Mom*.

Training is now a family affair. Her husband, Joshua Gomez, was a top-ranked amateur middleweight boxer. Now, he's her training partner, padded up to take her blows. Her goal is to be the first UFC champion who is also a mom.

"I'm a non-confrontational person. There is almost always a non-violent resolution to any situation."

—*Michelle Waterson*

Liane Lissa Sato

Do you think that being taller would make you a better volleyball player? At five feet, three and a half inches, Liane Sato was usually the shortest person on the court, but she made up for her lack of height with her speed and defensive skills. They earned her a place on two Olympic volleyball teams.

Liane Sato won a bronze medal as part of the USA Volleyball team at the 1992 Olympics in Barcelona, Spain. She also competed in the 1988 Summer Olympics, where her team finished in seventh place. With all five children in her family playing Division I volleyball and three representing the United States in international competitions, Liane is the only girl in America's "First Family of Volleyball."

Liane's parents, Richard and Elissa Sato, were avid recreational volleyball players in their youth. Elissa preferred sports over television for her children's entertainment. She would send them to John Adams Middle School gym in Santa Monica, California, to play volleyball after they finished their homework. The family also played volleyball at the beach together. The 1988 Seoul Summer Olympics and the 1992 Barcelona Olympics were also a family affair. All seven members of the Sato family attended both Olympics. Not only was Liane on the U.S. women's team, but Liane's brother Eric made the U.S. men's team, which their brother Gary coached.

After the 1992 Olympics, Liane switched to professional beach volleyball. From 1994 to 1995, she was the captain of Team Paul Mitchell for the Four-Women Pro Beach Tour.

She now teaches and coaches at her California alma mater, Santa Monica High School. She led both her boys' and girls' teams to California Interscholastic Federation victories. Liane passes on her family's legacy of hard work, team building, and success as a role model, coach, and teacher to the next generation.

"My generation grew up playing on the beach because we could walk there, it was free and beach doubles is an exciting and dynamic game to watch."

—*Liane Sato*

She might be the shortest player on the volleyball court, but she used her speed and skill to compete at the highest level.

Catherine Mai-Lan Fox

As a young girl, Catherine Fox had fantasies of Olympic gold. Little did she realize that she would become a two-time Olympic gold medal winner for swimming. Catherine's parents, Tom Fox and To Kim Hoa, met in Vietnam during the Vietnam War. Her father, an American, was a reporter for the *New York Times*. Her mother was a Vietnamese social worker. They married and relocated to the United States, first to Detroit, Michigan, and then to Kansas City, Kansas.

Catherine began swimming at age 7 and joined the Kansas City Blazers at 11. After a few years, she started to train seriously, swimming 30 hours a week in pursuit of her goal of making the Olympic team. At five feet, six inches, she focused on technique to make up for the advantage that taller opponents had in wingspan. Her fast starts and turns, along with her underwater undulation, proved effective. She was part of the 400-meter freestyle and medley relays at the 1996 Atlanta Olympics, taking home two gold medals. At Stanford University, she was a 12-time All American and a 9-time NCAA champion.

Megan Khang

Megan Khang is the first Hmong American to compete in the Ladies Professional Golf Association (LPGA). She turned professional at 18 after earning her tour card on her first attempt.

Megan's parents, Lee and Nou Khang, both fled Laos in 1975 as children during the Vietnam War. Both Lee and Nou made their way to Thailand, where they lived in refugee camps before immigrating to the United States.

Megan's father, Lee, taught himself to play golf at age 32 by reading golf magazines and watching YouTube videos. He introduced Megan to golf when she was five years old. She dominated junior amateur golf, qualifying to play in three of four U.S. Women's Opens. She was just 14 when she qualified for the first one in 2012, and she also competed in 2014 and 2015.

Though heavily recruited for college golf scholarships, Megan decided to forgo college and to compete professionally instead. She was one of only five teenagers to earn her LPGA card in 2016. With her family by her side, Megan has begun a journey of success borne of sacrifice and love for the game.

Mohini Bhardwaj

Mohini Bhardwaj is the first Indian American gymnast to medal at the Olympics, winning silver at the 2004 Summer Olympics in Athens.

Mohini was born in Philadelphia on September 29, 1978. Her mother, Indu, is a Russian from New York, and her father, Kaushal, is from India. Mohini started gymnastic classes at age four. In search of better coaching, Mohini moved to Orlando at age 14 to train at Brown's Gymnastics. Two years later, she moved on her own to Houston in the hope of making the 1996 Olympic team.

At the Olympic trials in Boston, Mohini missed the cut by a mere .075 point. She left elite gymnastics in 1998 to attend UCLA on a full gymnastics scholarship. Success at the collegiate level fueled her desire to make the 2004 Olympic team.

As the last-second replacement for an injured teammate, Mohini was called up to compete on the balance beam in the Olympic team final with just five minutes' notice. Mohini nailed her routine and the United States won silver.

Naomi Osaka

Naomi Osaka is the first female Asian player to hold the No. 1 ranking by the Women's Tennis Association (WTA). She earned this ranking at age 21 by winning five titles, including two grand slam singles titles, the 2019 Australian Open, and the 2018 U.S. Open.

Naomi was born in Osaka, Japan, to Leonard Maxine Francois, who is Haitian, and Tamaki Osaka, who is Japanese. When she was three years old, her family moved to New York. Naomi played tennis during the day and was homeschooled at night. In 2006, the family moved to Florida to focus on tennis. Naomi turned professional in September 2013. At age 16, she defeated U.S. Open champion Samantha Stosur at the 2014 Stanford Classic. This win would mark the beginning of her ascent to the No. 1 ranking.

A dual citizen of Japan and the United States, Naomi chose to represent Japan under a 1985 Japanese law that requires dual citizens to renounce one of their citizenships before their 22nd birthday. She is Japan's first female tennis player to win a grand slam title.

To Learn More About Each Athlete

https://charactermedia.com/april-cover-story-e-j-ok-is-one-of-the-greatest-point-guards-you-never-heard-of/

https://bleacherreport.com/articles/2754663-chloe-kim-is-just-getting-started

Burfoot, Amby. *First Ladies of Running: 22 Inspiring Profiles of the Rebels, Rule Breakers, and Visionaries Who Changed the Sport Forever.* Emmaus: Rodale, 2016.

https://brokeassstuart.com/2017/11/02/sfcentric-history-filipino-american-vicki-draves-made-olympic-history/

https://ishof.org/soichi-sakamoto.html

https://news.harvard.edu/gazette/story/2007/06/chu-on-harvard-i-wish-i-could-stay-here-forever/

http://beatsandrhymesfc.com/natasha-kai-interview-bring-the-beat-back-sky-blues-hawaiian-returns-to-rock-the-house/

https://www.espn.com/espnw/news-commentary/story/_/id/13195191/how-michelle-wie-story-makes-us-rethink-meaning-success

https://www.deseret.com/1992/2/8/18966400/mature-yamaguchi-is-out-for-gold-br

https://www.pdsoros.org/news-events/2016/08/03/amy-chow-olympian-physician-and-2003-paul-daisy-soros-fellow

https://generations808.com/ko-a-moana-those-of-the-ocean/

Gay, Nancy. *Know the Fighter: Michelle Waterson.* Amazon Services, 2017.

https://www.surfsantamonica.com/ssm_site/the_lookout/news/news-2011/april-2011/04_01_2011_volleyball_legends_the_sato_family_inducted_into_smc_sports_hall_of_fame.html

https://www.usaswimming.org/news/2018/04/26/catherine-fox-is-finding-and-giving-balance-to-life

https://www.golfchannel.com/news/megan-khangs-remarkable-journey-solheim-cup-began-parents-during-vietnam-war

https://www.flogymnastics.com/articles/5041352-legend-spotlight-with-mohini-bhardwaj-barry

https://www.theringer.com/2018/12/21/18150938/naomi-osaka-tennis-future-identity-year-in-review

About the Author

Mia Wenjen blogs on children's books and parenting at PragmaticMom.com. She is also the co-creator of Multicultural Children's Book Day, a nonprofit celebrating diversity in children's books. She has written *Asian Pacific American Heroes*, picture book *Sumo Joe, The Elusive Full Ride Scholarship: An Insider's Guide,* and *How to Coach Girls,* which won a Silver IBPA Benjamin Franklin Award. Mia lives in Boston with her husband, three kids, and a golden retriever.

63857322R00020